Charlotte Sebag-Montefiore

RIDDLES FROM THE SEA
Who am I?

Bumblebee Books
London

A CIP catalogue record for this title is
available from the British Library.

ISBN: 978-1-83934-363-6

Bumblebee Books is an imprint of
Olympia Publishers.

First Published in 2021

Bumblebee Books
Tallis House
2 Tallis Street
London
EC4Y 0AB

Printed in Great Britain

www.olympiapublishers.com

Dedication

To my dear grandchildren,
Lily, Hannah, Flora and Moshe.

1

We're mammals and we must breathe air.
That is the reason why
we can't stay long beneath the waves,
or we will surely die!

We need a lot of fish to eat,
swim mostly in the sea.
We're very clever. I do hope
you'll come and play with me!

Our tummies mostly have three parts.
We swallow our prey whole.
We have got teeth but do not chew,
we breathe through our blow-hole.

Our sight and hearing's very good,
we have no sense of smell.
We're really very social,
alone we don't do well.

We live together in a pod,
perhaps a thousand strong.
That's a safer way to hunt and play,
we do that all day long.

Now that you have listened,
just tell me, what's my name.
If you don't know don't worry
I'll tell you all the same!

2

We've colonies, we're flightless birds.
We're often in the sea.
We're not afraid of people,
you're not afraid of me!

We swim so fast we nearly fly
in fact, we simply leap.
We can drink salty water
and we really dive quite deep.

We cannot run away on land,
we've flippers but no feet!
They help us swim fast in the sea
where there is fish to eat!

Our beaks and tongues have useful spines
to grip our wriggling prey.
The spines we have prevent the fish
from slipping right away.

Our chicks must stay upon the land,
they must stay nice and dry.
Their feathers are not waterproof,
that is the reason why!

Now that you have listened,
just tell me, what's my name.
If you don't know don't worry
I'll tell you all the same!

3

Some people think that we look like
a flower from the land.
Some of us attach ourselves
to rocks quite near the sand!

My mouth is on my bottom,
that is a funny place.
It has to be that way because
I haven't got a face!

Most of us like warmer seas.
My tentacles can sting.
Even if they're really bleached,
they sting like anything!

Some of us can move about
slowly, and not fast.
Like a slug does on the land,
we do arrive at last!

Little shrimps may clean us up,
a cleaning operation.
We protect them from their predators,
this is co-operation!

Now that you have listened,
just tell me, what's my name.
If you don't know don't worry
I'll tell you all the same!

4

We can heat our brain and eyes,
it does improve our vision.
This helps us hunt and kill for food
which we do with precision!

We slash our prey from side to side
to injure our next meal!
When hurt, our victim must slow down,
that's a help to us, we feel!

We do not swim in shoals or schools,
we hunt alone at night.
We're powerful, and if sharks attack,
they face a fearsome fight!

My bill extends quite like a sword.
For teeth, I have no need.
I swallow my prey whole, you see,
a giant gulp indeed!

We're often nearly ten feet long,
girls longer than the male.
We're very good as swimmers,
two arms make up our tail!

Now that you have listened,
just tell me, what's my name.
If you don't know don't worry
I'll tell you all the same!

5

Twice a year my beak will change.
That is just my way.
From winter grey to orange
on a lovely summer's day!

I flap and flap and flap my wings
and really fly quite fast.
When I'm tired, I rest on waves
and watch my world float past!

I'm very good at swimming
and dive deep down at sea
to catch a scrumptious, yummy fish
and eat it for my tea!

I and my faithful loving mate
work hard to build our nest.
We live in noisy colonies
together with the rest!

We have a single egg each year.
It takes six weeks to hatch it.
We sit and watch until it does,
a gull might come and snatch it!

Now that you have listened,
just tell me, what's my name.
If you don't know don't worry
I'll tell you all the same!

6

I'm afraid I'm so delicious
that you use me as bait.
To catch the cod you like so much
– alas, that is my fate!

I have a beak you can't digest,
I've lovely blood that's blue.
I have three hearts which does exceed
the one that's owned by you!

I do glow brightly in the dark,
deep down there in the sea.
I have enormous giant eyes
that are just right for me!

When fully grown, our girls
are bigger than the boys.
We're intelligent and clever,
we do not like much noise.

I've eight arms and two tentacles,
we attack with speed, spray ink
we eat fish and each other,
and that is all, I think!

Now that you have listened,
just tell me, what's my name.
If you don't know don't worry
I'll tell you all the same!

7

My teeth are in my stomach,
my brain is very small.
When you cook me, I turn red.
I don't grow very tall.

I hide in rocks and crevices,
I could be yellow, blue or white.
I've lots and lots of predators,
I'm active in the night!

I've legs aplenty, ten of them.
A runner I'll never be.
My claws could break your fingers
at the deep end of the sea.

My shell is tough, protects me.
Inside, I'm good to eat.
For many I am tasty,
I am protein, I am meat.

My shell comes off from time to time,
no room in there to grow.
When it's off, I eat it
for the calcium, you know!

Now that you have listened,
just tell me, what's my name.
If you don't know don't worry
I'll tell you all the same!

8

My wings outstretch the other birds.
I like to fly by day.
A single trip, ten thousand miles,
– oh yes, that is my way!

I catch the wind and soar aloft,
then downwards I do drift.
I barely need to flap my wings
the air just gives me lift!

Danger comes if I should float
and rest upon the sea.
Tiger sharks may swim along
and have a feast on me!

Food and flight are easier
with climate change and winds.
But if the wind speed gets too much,
trouble then begins!

Longline fishing hooks and nets
are dangerous for me too.
I may get tangled up in them,
the threat to me from you!

Now that you have listened,
just tell me, what's my name.
If you don't know don't worry
I'll tell you all the same!

9

We lay a lot of eggs,
a million, if we can.
We need to, for you've eaten us
since you lot began!

We certainly can help you
keep the water clean
by filtering gallons every hour,
if you see what I mean!

If a tiny grain of sand should
penetrate my shell,
it will become a lovely pearl,
pale, rose, or black as well!

My body is quite strange.
We change our sex a lot.
Three chambers to my heart,
that is what I've got!

We help prevent erosion
In many different ways.
We helped the Greeks to count their votes
in far off ancient days!

Now that you have listened,
just tell me, what's my name.
If you don't know don't worry
I'll tell you all the same!

10

You may think that we just eat fish
but this is just not true.
We swallow birds, turtles and shrimps,
though we do not eat you!

The pouch that dangles from our bill
helps us catch our prey.
But I think it nets us more
– that simply is our way!

My feet are webbed – we're water birds,
we have four useful toes.
We like to breathe in through our mouth,
we close our lovely nose!

Our nose is used to purge us
of the salt that's in the sea.
Too much salt is just not good
for you or indeed me!

We sometimes hunt in groups.
It's effective and more fun.
We gather fish together
and we eat it when we're done!

Now that you have listened,
just tell me, what's my name.
If you don't know don't worry
I'll tell you all the same!

11

Our name describes the way I look.
Our home: seas north and south.
All of us have got two tums
and one comes through our mouth!

I've spines on top, and loads of feet,
I've no gills nor a fin.
I open out the mussel shells,
I'm protected by tough skin.

I have five arms that stick right out,
I have no brain or blood.
I'm not a fish, no head, you see.
I like the sandy mud!

I cannot see in detail.
I do know light from dark.
I sometimes lose an arm or two
escaping from a shark!

It takes a while to grow it back
and then I am like new.
Humans can't regenerate,
I'm glad I'm not like you!

Now that you have listened,
just tell me, what's my name.
If you don't know don't worry
I'll tell you all the same!

12

Camouflage is useful
to hide me in the sea.
I may be transparent
then you won't be eating me!

I'm good at swimming forwards,
I use my swimmerets.
They are like legs in pairs, you see.
I try to avoid nets!

If it's backwards I must go,
my tail will flick and flick.
This is what I need to do
to swim back very quick!

Sometimes we dance to bring fish close,
we clean them up, you see!
They do not eat us and we munch
their parasites for tea!

We eat small plants and animals,
mostly alive, some dead!
My heart is in a funny place,
you'll find it in my head!

Now that you have listened,
just tell me, what's my name.
If you don't know don't worry
I'll tell you all the same!

13

We live in all the oceans
that there are throughout the world.
I'm never straight or stretched, you know,
but wavy, maybe curled.

Our reach can really be quite long.
Swimmers should get out,
before they get a nasty sting
from our tentacles about!

If you put me on the beach
or somewhere on the land,
in several hours, I'll only be
a shadow on the sand!

I'm not clever (I've no brain),
I do have eyes galore
to see about me as I need.
I may have twenty-four!

Some of us have eight arms
to bring us food that squirms.
Plankton maybe, little fish,
or sometimes prawns or worms!

Now that you have listened,
just tell me, what's my name.
If you don't know don't worry
I'll tell you all the same!

14

In springtime, we are near the shore,
in autumn further out.
Deep down in the oceans,
that's where we swim about!

You people have red arrows
that keep in strict formation.
We fishes have another way
as befits our station!

Our wavy stripes are useful
to keep our shoal in line,
our speed must be the same, you see,
we must learn to align!

Our life is hard. For bigger fish
we are a tasty prey.
Our eggs are mostly eaten up,
that is nature's way!

Our flesh is very healthy
with oils, Omega-3.
A reason why you like us
when you do lunch on me!

Now that you have listened,
just tell me, what's my name.
If you don't know don't worry
I'll tell you all the same!

15

All of us have tusks for teeth,
they aren't just for the boys.
We like the cold seas of the north,
we take fright if there's noise.

Stampeding really is no joke,
our calves may even die.
Our eyesight's poor, we might fall off
a cliff and not know why!

Mustachio'd, with whiskers,
hundreds, you should know.
They're sensitive and help us find
our food, so down we go!

Right down to the ocean floor
– we like a shallow sea.
We hold our breath for half an hour
to find food for our tea!

Sea cucumbers and mussels
that's what we like to eat.
Clams as well, soft coral
and how we like some meat!

Now that you have listened,
just tell me, what's my name.
If you don't know don't worry
I'll tell you all the same!

16

I'm fearsome and ferocious,
my sharp fangs face each way.
I have a very nasty bite,
I gobble up my prey!

Thirty miles an hour and more,
that is my swimming speed.
I can produce an extra spurt
to catch the fish I need!

I like warm salty water,
I can reach six feet long.
You think I taste delicious,
I'm muscular and strong.

I can be black, brown grey or blue,
I may have some dark spots.
I ambush fish, surprise them,
we must catch lots and lots!

When you're diving in the sea,
be careful, I might bite.
You see we like the way you taste.
My hunting time's the night!

Now that you have listened,
just tell me, what's my name.
If you don't know don't worry
I'll tell you all the same!

17

I'm a reptile, I breathe air
though I do live in the sea.
Most of us are pretty long,
five foot or more, maybe.

To swim, I simply wriggle.
I am not a fish.
You will not hear me coming,
as silently I swish!

Our young are born alive
somewhere in the sea.
Up to twenty at a time,
they slither out of me!

Crocodiles and sharks
make me panic with sheer fright.
I'm never safe: they go for me,
attacking day and night.

We can hold our breath two hours,
sometimes even three.
We can be highly poisonous,
– don't you mess with me.

Now that you have listened,
just tell me, what's my name.
If you don't know don't worry
I'll tell you all the same!

18

You'll know me by my eight long limbs,
my tentacles as well.
They help me get the food I need,
oh, I eat very well.

Sharks and whales and even birds,
dolphins and large fish,
hunt and want to eat me up,
I am their tasty dish!

I wriggle into places,
just the size for me.
They cannot fit, we spray our ink
so that they cannot see!

I have three hearts, a bird-sized brain,
I really like to play!
My eyesight and my sense of touch
are good, I'm glad to say!

My arms are really very strong,
they shift stones as building blocks.
When I squeeze into tight spaces,
they can make a door from rocks!

Now that you have listened,
just tell me, what's my name.
If you don't know don't worry
I'll tell you all the same!

19

I like to live in herds
on the bottom of the sea.
Shallow, deep or coral reefs,
it doesn't bother me!

I eat what others leave,
detritus, as they say.
I clear the acid, clean things up,
that is just my way.

I can be orange, red or brown.
I do not breathe like you.
I can't, you see, I have no nose
that I can breathe right through!

My body's soft and tubular.
I send out sticky threads
that trap and snare my predators,
I wind it round their heads!

In Asia, humans eat me if they can.
I do fetch quite a price.
It's a pity that you like me so,
and find me very nice!

Now that you have listened,
just tell me, what's my name.
If you don't know don't worry
I'll tell you all the same!

20

We lived here with the dinosaurs,
reptiles from long ago.
My shell grows with me, keeps me safe,
protects me, did you know?

I can live twice as long as you.
Some of us eat meat.
Jellyfish and squid and things,
you think we're good to eat!

We lay our eggs upon the beach
in a lovely, pleasant spot.
Some of us lay hundreds,
but some of us do not!

We hide our eggs as best we can,
we hope they will survive.
In ten weeks' time, or maybe less
that they will hatch alive!

In some of us, the temperature
determines what we'll be.
A boy if it is colder,
if it's warm, a girl we'll see!

Now that you have listened,
just tell me, what's my name.
If you don't know don't worry
I'll tell you all the same!

21

I live throughout our lovely world
in waters cold and warm.
I've fins and gills, no tummy though,
for us this is the norm!

I'm not the sort of horse you ride,
I can't swim very well.
I tie my tail to seaweed
to hold against the swell.

I can change my colour,
then I can't be seen.
Camouflage is useful,
I can be grey or green!

My dad has got a breeding pouch,
eggs in hundreds stay some weeks.
Then he shoots the babies out,
that's what my mother seeks!

My mum and dad are faithful.
Each and every day,
they link their tails and twirl around,
singing in their way!

Now that you have listened,
just tell me, what's my name.
If you don't know don't worry
I'll tell you all the same!

22

We are five hundred different kinds,
we're from the ancient past.
We are in all the oceans,
oh, we were built to last.

We are the cleverest of fish,
our skin is rough and thick.
We sense our prey electrically,
we go for it so quick!

Our teeth wear out with all we chew
but we grow thousands more!
Then we tear off chunks of meat
just as we did before!

We need to stay awake to breathe.
We hear the slightest sound.
Our eyes are placed so they can look
and really see all round!

At swimming, we are really great,
but we are jumpers too.
To catch our prey, we need this skill,
we rarely go for you.

Now that you have listened,
just tell me, what's my name.
If you don't know don't worry
I'll tell you all the same!

23

We mostly like a warmer sea,
quite shallow, not too deep.
Small animals in colonies,
we pile up in a heap!

We clean water. If it is too hot,
we may just bleach and die.
It's awful as we matter,
I'm going to tell you why!

We protect you from the waves,
I don't know if you knew!
Our fish feeds half a billion
people, just like you!

We're useful in your medicine,
for arthritis, cancer heart.
Who would think that we
would play such a useful part?

Marine life, yes, a quarter
is what we help to thrive.
We are vital in the struggle
to keep it all alive!

Now that you have listened,
just tell me, what's my name.
If you don't know don't worry
I'll tell you all the same!

24

I swim much faster than a seal.
I meet my friends for sleep.
Mammals in a humpy pile,
we make a lovely heap!

Unlike the seal, when we molt
we can still dive and fish.
We swallow them, sometimes whole.
Stream-lined we simply swish!

We use our ear flaps to keep warm.
They heat and catch the sun.
If we're too hot, we open down,
that is how it's done!

There's another way our ear flaps help,
They keep the water out
when we're swimming underneath,
going round about!

I hold my breath a long, long time.
The oxygen, you see,
stays in my heart while I go deep.
A diver, yes, that's me!

Now that you have listened,
just tell me, what's my name.
If you don't know don't worry
I'll tell you all the same!

25

I have a secret weapon
which I use to stun my prey.
I have to have some food, don't I?
I do it, anyway.

I could even knock you out
though you are so much bigger.
I simply shoot, and do not even
have to pull the trigger!

Some of us do grow quite big,
some fourteen feet in length.
Being made of cartilage,
that means we have great strength.

I don't fuss over water,
it may be shallow or quite deep!
I'm sluggish and slow moving,
I do not jump or leap!

We come all different colours,
blend in and lie in wait,
an ambush, till our prey comes by
to meet its death and fate!

Now that you have listened,
just tell me, what's my name.
If you don't know don't worry
I'll tell you all the same!

26

I've cousins in fresh water
but I prefer the sea.
Somewhere nice and salty,
don't come close to me.

I can swim in the ocean
but mostly near the land.
In quiet coastal shallows,
somewhere near the sand.

I'm fearsome in the water,
I can even climb a tree.
And I run faster than you think
no one's safe with me.

I lurk beneath, my eyes above,
I do not share my prey.
I am the biggest reptile,
I eat what comes my way!

In Queensland, in Australia,
in the North and West,
we can even eat a shark,
as hunters, we're the best!

Now that you have listened,
just tell me, what's my name.
If you don't know don't worry
I'll tell you all the same!

27

You might think I'm not social,
but this is not quite right.
I like to be with my own kind,
I'm active in the night!

I have to shed my shell at times
but move into another.
Maybe, who knows, it once belonged
to my sister or my brother!

My pincers are so useful.
They're like a knife and fork.
They help me climb, defend myself,
they take me for a walk!

The anemone protects me,
at least that is my plan.
It gives my predators a sting,
I feed it if I can!

If it's quiet and salty,
I can hear quite well.
We hear sound through vibrations
and I can also smell.

Now that you have listened,
just tell me, what's my name.
If you don't know don't worry
I'll tell you all the same!

28

I have no waist, I'm tapered,
fat helps me keep afloat.
I'm a mammal and a swimmer,
you prize my furry coat.

We are found in polar seas,
and in some others too.
Our predators are whales and sharks,
polar bears and you!

We ourselves are carnivores
and like a meal of fish,
other seals and birds at sea
all make a tasty dish!

Our whiskers help us find our prey.
We've useful strong webbed feet.
Together with our sense of smell,
they help us find our meat!

We dive down and close our nose
for half an hour or so.
Some of us for twice as long
if we need to stay below!

Now that you have listened,
just tell me, what's my name.
If you don't know don't worry
I'll tell you all the same!

29

I'm different from a sea snake
because I've got a fin.
Some of us live in the sea,
That is what we live in!

I am a skilful swimmer,
swimming backwards which is rare.
Which way the waves are going
makes no difference, I don't care!

We can be hard to find.
We're most active in the night.
We may burrow in the sand,
though some go deep alright.

At night we like the warmer seas,
at dawn we dive down deep.
We spend the day there, then come up
to hunt and pounce and leap!

Our journey is the same each year,
to the far Sargasso Sea.
It suits us there to spawn our young,
it's a long way though, for me!

Now that you have listened,
just tell me, what's my name.
If you don't know don't worry
I'll tell you all the same!

30

When I'm born, my skin is bare.
Then down and feathers show.
I'm blind a while, so Mum and Dad
take care of me, you know!

A long time, we stay in our nest,
more than fifty days.
Then we join a nice large flock,
learn flight and bird-like ways!

We stretch our neck, and beat our wings
so rapidly, they flap.
At night, we find a cliff or reeds
and there we take a nap!

We're excellent at swimming,
dive deep, a hundred feet.
We're seabirds but we do prefer
freshwater birds for meat!

Some people tie cords round our neck,
that is what you do.
We cannot swallow what we catch
we give it all to you!

Now that you have listened,
just tell me, what's my name.
If you don't know don't worry
I'll tell you all the same!

31

A shell, a darting tongue, a fin
and brains, oh that is me.
I can learn to find my way
through mazes in the sea!

Some of us can walk
upon the ocean floor.
You will not find us coming
round to you next door!

Camouflage is useful
to escape, I change my skin.
This can help another way,
it draws the ladies in!

Sometimes I may try to pass
for a female of my kind.
Then, you see, my needs are met.
The girls don't seem to mind!

A nasty vicious predator,
I deal with in my way.
I stun it with a show of lights
and then enjoy my day!

Now that you have listened,
just tell me, what's my name.
If you don't know don't worry
I'll tell you all the same!

32

We are a tip-top predator
and mammals just like you.
We're sociable and live in packs,
teach our young what to do.

We love our mums, and stay with them,
our girls, their daughters too.
Our descent line is through mothers,
that is quite rare with you.

All the same our males
choose partners from elsewhere.
It's better for the genes, it is,
that they swim off somewhere!

We sometimes sleep when diving,
we sleep with half our brain.
So we know when to surface
and rise for air again!

We even have a dialect
as we vocalize and call.
It's special to our group, you see,
not a language for us all!

Now that you have listened,
just tell me, what's my name.
If you don't know don't worry
I'll tell you all the same!

33

I do not swim in water,
I like to cling to rocks.
We just go together,
as shoes do with their socks!

I have threads which attach me,
you use them in a glue.
They really help me stick to things,
they stick in surgery too!

Many creatures eat me
that's why my shell is tough.
But some just crack it open,
it is not tough enough!

We work so hard to get our food.
Filtering all day
for plankton, tiny animals,
that is just our way!

We simply are delicious
and very good to eat.
With minerals and proteins
and our lovely tasty meat!

Now that you have listened,
just tell me, what's my name.
If you don't know don't worry
I'll tell you all the same!

34

Our numbers are declining.
We choose our nests with care,
building them on islands, dunes,
cliffs, hard to reach somewhere!

We're omnivores and clever,
eat seeds, a fish, a worm.
We stamp our feet when in a group,
so earthworms rise and squirm!

Our children learn and copy us.
We pass on what we know,
like opening shells by dropping them
onto the rocks below.

Rearing chicks is difficult.
There are many tasks to share.
We feed, protect them till they're grown,
we're parents who both care.

We take the gifts on offer,
food if it's about,
the blowing wind to help us fly
somewhere when we're out!

Now that you have listened,
just tell me, what's my name.
If you don't know don't worry
I'll tell you all the same!

35

Some of us live on the land
and some live in the sea.
Whichever, our gills must stay moist
a little tail, that's me!

My shell keeps me nice and safe,
my teeth are in my tummy.
I eat whatever I can get
I don't fuss, it's all yummy!

I do feel pain, I'm sad to say.
I wish that I did not.
When you boil me up for lunch,
it hurts me such a lot!

A decapod, that means ten legs,
we communicate our way.
We flap our pincers, drum our claws,
that's how we have our say!

You'll know me by my sideways walk.
I do not work alone.
This helps me feed my family,
I'm not much on my own!

Now that you have listened,
just tell me, what's my name.
If you don't know don't worry
I'll tell you all the same!

36

I like to live somewhere that's warm.
A torpedo in my shape,
a tail that's forked is what I have,
this all helps me escape.

My fins have dual function
it's very useful too.
They spread and serve as wings outstretched,
I am so glad they do!

A dark blue on the top,
a silver gleam below.
I swim when I am in the sea,
glide in the air, you know.

In the air, my predators
are birds, they chase me too.
At sea, it's mackerel, tuna,
– the swordfish, also you.

I may jump in your boat,
you attract me using light.
So I cause my own undoing.
I like to eat at night!

Now that you have listened,
just tell me, what's my name.
If you don't know don't worry
I'll tell you all the same!

Answers

1. Dolphin
2. Penguin
3. Sea Anemone
4. Swordfish
5. Puffin
6. Squid
7. Lobster
8. Albatross
9. Oyster
10. Pelican
11. Starfish
12. Shrimp
13. Jellyfish
14. Mackerel
15. Walrus
16. Barracuda
17. Sea Snake
18. Octopus
19. Sea Cucumber
20. Turtle
21. Sea Horse
22. Shark
23. Coral
24. Sea Lion
25. Electric ray
26. Sea Crocodile
27. Hermit Crab
28. Seal
29. Eel
30. Cormorant
31. Cuttlefish
32. Orca
33. Mussel
34. Sea gull
35. Crab
36. Flying fish

About the Author

Charlotte Sebag-Montefiore's many years of experience as a clinical psychologist in the NHS, and as a mother and grandmother, has helped her produce books which children love. Charlotte loves dinosaurs and animals – they are so interesting! And Charlotte really enjoys rhymes and riddles!

Her first two books, *WHO AM I?* and *MORE ANIMAL RIDDLES* combined her interest in animals, with her love of rhyme and riddles. Her third book *HERBIE AND THE T. REX* is the start of a dinosaur world, where the different dinosaur characters each deal with the issues confronting them in their own way.

She returned to riddles and rhyme with this book, as she cannot resist them!

Acknowledgements

I would like to acknowledge the constant support my husband has given me, and also, the valuable advice and support I have received from Chantelle Wadsworth.